Private Stories
Monologues for Young Actors
Ages 8 to 16

Private Stories
Monologues for Young Actors Ages 8 to 16

and the
Seven Key Questions to Unlock Your Imagination

Elizabeth Bauman

Limelight Editions
An Imprint of Hal Leonard Corporation
New York

Limelight Editions (an imprint of Hal Leonard Corporation)
19 West 21st Street, New York, NY 10010

First published by Limelight Editions in 2007

Originally published in 2005

Printed in the United States of America

Library of Congress Cataloging-in-Publication Data is available upon request.

ISBN-10: 0-87910-341-8
ISBN-13: 978-0-87910-341-5

www.limelighteditions.com

CONTENTS

ACKNOWLEDGMENTS

I wish to thank all my students from over the years for trusting and honoring me with the truth of their lives. Thank you to those at the Lee Strasberg Theatre and Film Institute, Anna Strasberg, Laurel Long, and my fellow teachers. A special thank-you to Deborah Solis for her amazing help editing this book.

Thank you to Claudette Sutherland for her wonderful editing help. Thank you to Barney Cheng for his generous help with my final edits. Thank you to Professor Pam Dunn, founder of the Drama Therapy Institute of Los Angeles, John Raasch, Pam Paulson, Karen Early, Ellen Spindel, Kerry Muir and Mac Muir-Jeffries, Charlie Dierkop, Carol Weiss, Geraldine Baron, and Blake Gibbons.

A special thank you to my beautiful father, Martin Bauman, for being such an extraordinary example of success in spite of adversity and for his unconditional love.

A very special thank you to Max Bougrov, Alan Cooper, Melia Duerksen, Justin Hawkins, Hannah Rose Kramer, Tatiana Marchant, Garland McCutcheon, and Michael Perez. These children participated in the first workshop production of *Private Stories* in the Marilyn Monroe Theatre at the Lee Strasberg Theatre and Film Institute, Los Angeles.

PREFACE

In 1996, I was teaching at the All About Kids Acting Conservatory. At that time, I was picking materials for the young actors in my class, but I noticed little or nothing was written about the process of helping a new young actor connect to material. There were many interesting monologue books, but I couldn't find one that simply breaks down the acting process for a young person.

During one of my classes, I gave one of my nine-year-old students, Damon, a monologue to read. The monologue had to do with losing a best friend. He read it, but it sounded flat, unreal, and speech-like.

"Did anything like this ever happen to you?"

"No."

"How do you think the person in the story feels?"

"I don't know."

"Guess."

Damon shrugged and looked at me blankly.

"There is no right or wrong answer," I assured him. "Just what you think and feel."

Then, I noticed his new basketball sneakers.

"Those are great sneakers!"

He smiled and came alive as he admired the sneakers.

"Did you just get them?"

"Yeah, my dad took me shopping Friday."

"You like basketball?"

"Oh, yes. Scotty Pippin is the best. Me and my best friend watch all his games."

"What is your best friend's name?"

"Eli."

"Why is he your best friend?"

"Because he makes me laugh. We like all the same things, and he always has my back."

"Would you be upset if he moved away?"

"Oh, that would be the worst."

"Why?"

"I would be totally alone; I could never find another friend like Eli, ever."

"Okay, would you read the monologue again, please?"

Damon then read the monologue again. His energy shifted, his words came alive, and images he described became more real. All Damon needed was something he could relate to or care about to spark his imagination for the monologue. I decided that was how I would work with young people new to acting.

I wrote this book to provide fresh material with universal themes. I also wanted to give young actors simple tools so they could learn to work on their own. By asking seven simple questions, they can begin to create unique, well-rounded characters completely from their imagination.

Sometimes it's not easy for an actor to create a character or situation outside his or her experience. Therefore, when writing a monologue, I sometimes take an experience, issue, or situation from the student's own life and create a fictional story around it. This way, students can immediately relate to the material and more easily connect to the parts that are not of their experience. This process widens their empathy and enables them to step into another person's shoes using their imagination. It also helps them to begin to create a non-literal reality.

A child experiences joy, love, confusion, or fear much like an adult. However, the circumstances and development change with age. When a young child experiences fear of loss or love for the first time, he or she needs a supportive, safe, and nurturing environment in which to validate and express those emotions. Reading and performing monologues dealing with different emotions and experiences enrich a young person's development. By performing monologues with these age-appropriate issues in front of peers, young people learn they are not alone.

For eight years, I have been teaching children from the age of six to young adults up to eighteen. My classes begin with students sitting in a circle and sharing whatever is on their mind. This encourages students to express themselves confidently and comfortably among their peers. Students share their experiences, listen to one another's stories and offer advice. They learn that everyone faces similar issues and problems. This sharing time not only strengthens the bonds among the students but also builds communicating and listening skills.

Instead of always assigning the monologues, I give students the chance to choose materials that appeal to them. They choose from plays, monologue books, or pieces that I have written tailor-made for the students mostly based on the sharing time. To enhance and open channels for creativity, I play the music of Mozart softly in the background while the students choose and read pieces of interest for about thirty minutes. Then they read their selections on stage, giving and receiving feedback. They choose a monologue that speaks to them. For the next eight weeks, they work on it. This culminates in a performance at the end of the eight-week session.

I believe a young person gets disconnected to an extent during socialization, as well as from the excessive stress from school. Young people are bombarded on a daily basis with issues of "belonging" outside the classroom, and always having to know the "right answer" inside the classroom. They spend excessive hours on the computer, in chat rooms, e-mailing, and playing video games. All of these activities inhibit true self-expression and creativity. And most important, these activities handicap their ability to relate to others. They stifle the development of a young person's imagination. Because they are so out of the habit of expressing themselves truthfully with emotion and without fear of being judged, what ends up coming out is usually a fragment of what they are capable of expressing.

My goal as a teacher is to encourage the natural expression and imagination that may have gotten stifled and to help students discover their unique choice-making abilities. I ask simple questions to find out who a student is and what is important to him or her. Then I ask the seven simple, relevant and thought-provoking questions. By asking these questions and allowing them the time and space to answer, they work without the pressure of having the right answer. They begin to relate their own unique ideas about life into the character from the material they are working on. I help reunite students with their instincts, creative abilities, and unique choice-making process. I encourage them to use their imagination, to shift thoughts, feelings, and ideas in order to relate to characters outside of their own range of experience.

Whether a young person seeks to pursue a career as a professional actor or engages in acting for self-development, recreation, or therapeutic purposes, working with monologues is invaluable. Monologues are snapshots of a moment in life. Working on them stimulates imagination and nurtures healthy personal development. For teachers, this book would be a helpful guide in structuring a monologue class. For parents, this book gives helpful insights into the creative process of acting as well as providing new audition pieces for their young actors. And most important, this book gives young actors fresh materials for auditions, class work and tools to be able to work on their own.

NOTES TO THE ACTOR

When professional actors go off to do their "homework," they ask themselves certain questions. These questions are not usually introduced until an actor is older. I see no reason why young actors should not learn how to begin to work on their own. Young actors, too, should be given the tools to do their "acting homework" and know how to take responsibility for making their work better and more personal.

Acting a monologue is not just standing on a stage and giving a speech. You are painting a picture with what you say and do and taking the audience on your journey. It is always important to remember that a big part of acting is behavior. By behavior, I mean what the character is doing on stage. It helps to ask yourself, "If I never said the words of the monologue but were to act out what was happening silently—living the life of this person—what would I be doing?" Think about what the character is going through and let an activity come out of that, making interesting and personal choices. If you think about it, we all have conversations with ourselves in our heads all the time, and our actions often come out of our thoughts and feelings. Acting is the opposite—you get the words of the character first, and then you fill in the thoughts, feelings, and actions of the character you are playing until you understand that other person so well it is as though the words are your own. When you know the words by heart and make interesting choices and activities for your character, and it flows as if you and the character you developed are one, it is one of the most exciting experiences you will ever have. It is a most magical journey and one that teaches you how to better understand others from the inside out.

SEVEN KEY QUESTIONS

Who are you?

Who do you imagine this person to be, based on what the monologue says about this person and what he or she is living through?

Where are you?

Where is your character when he or she is saying the words of the monologue? If the words don't tell you, it is your choice to imagine the place and make it real for you, so the audience believes it too.

Why are you there?

Wherever you are right now, there is a reason. Example: In the bookstore, looking for new acting material; at school, because that is your job as a young person; at home, because that's where you live; at McDonald's, because you're hungry. So ask yourself first, "What would I be doing in the place the character is in?" Then, "Why do I think he or she is there right now?" If you are not sure, guess. It will probably be a great idea.

What happened right before?

Our actions (what we do) usually come out of what we have just done. For example, if the words from my monologue speak about a weird dream I just had, I may want to do the monologue lying down with my pillow and blanket. Or, since I just woke up, I may act out washing my face and brushing my teeth and hair, all the while thinking about and trying to remember the details of my dream and trying to figure out what it means while I drink my milk.

Who are you talking to?

Make a choice about whom you would be speaking to. It could be anyone or anything. Examples are: a best friend, an enemy, mother, father, dog, God, a stranger, yourself, the audience. It is your choice.

What do you want?

Sometimes when we tell someone a story it is because we just need them to listen or forgive us, understand us, or because we cannot hold it in, because it is just too painful, sad, confusing, funny, or exciting. So please consider what you want from the person or people to whom you are speaking.

What clothing (costume) or props do you need?
What do you imagine your character wearing and bringing on stage to help you paint your picture for the audience?

Remember, there is no right or wrong. Acting is very personal. Making interesting choices that only you would think of makes the monologue come alive, and it's fun, too. These are questions to help you. Use them only if you want to.

BOYS

SEVEN KEY QUESTIONS SAMPLE—ALBERT

<u>Who am I</u>? Who do you imagine Albert to be? Is he a cool kid? A loner?

<u>Where am I</u>? After reading this monologue, think back. When you were reading did you see this story like a movie in your mind? If so, where do you imagine Albert is while telling this story? An example could be his room.

<u>Why am I here</u>? Why do you think Albert is where he is? Example: Home in his room, because he lives there and is too sad to go anyplace else.

<u>What happened right before (the monologue)</u>? Right before Albert says these lines, maybe he just hung up the phone, cried, talked to his parents, took down streamers and party things.

<u>What do I want</u>? Albert cannot have what he wants. She is not coming back. That adds to his sadness and anger. Perhaps he wants the audience's understanding right now. What do you think?

<u>Who am I talking to</u>? Maybe Albert is talking to the audience to see if anyone has ever felt the way he has, to get answers, to warn other kids of how grown-ups don't always tell the truth.

<u>What costume or props do I need</u>? Maybe a phone (since he just got off a long conversation, and it makes him still feel close to her). A picture of Maria? Party favors? A cake with the candles blown out? Maybe Albert is wearing his coolest outfit.

ALBERT

You can't believe what happened. My girlfriend was supposed to come home today. She went to visit her family in the D.R. That's the Dominican Republic. I waited all day for her to call. I didn't even go to school. My parents are very cool that way. So finally at five o'clock the phone rings and I pick it up on the first ring. It's Maria. She's crying, and I ask her what's wrong. She tells me she's still there and she's not coming back. Her parents won't let her. It was some kind of trick. They had said it was just a vacation but they lied. She was hysterical, and hearing her like that made me cry, too. We were on the phone for a long time, like an hour, so we had to get off. Now I can't even cry or laugh or scream. I feel nothing and everything all at the same time. It's so weird; I love this girl and she loves me. This is the first time I have ever felt this way in my life. I don't know what I'm going to do. How can I live without her?

How could her parents lie to her like that? To both of us? It makes me never want to trust another adult again, ever. But then I look at my parents, and they are the coolest and actually my best friends. I want to go there and get her, but I know that's impossible. Some people search a lifetime for the love of their life and sometimes never find them. I found her at (*put in your age*).

I was planning a surprise party for her, and now this—the total opposite of what was supposed to happen. It makes me think that love is a dangerous thing. It can make you feel like you're in heaven, like anything is possible, and on the turn of a dime everything can go wrong. You think you can't bear another minute of being here on earth without that person. And you can't get to them. Any adult who would say kids don't understand what love is or that youth is wasted on the young should go back and re-read Romeo and Juliet.

EXTRA MONOLOGUE NOTES—ALBERT

SEVEN KEY QUESTIONS—MALCOLM

Who am I?

_____

_____

_____

Where am I?

_____

_____

_____

Why am I here?

_____

_____

_____

What happened right before (the monologue)?

_____

_____

_____

What do I want?

_____

_____

_____

Who am I talking to?

_____

_____

_____

What costume or props do I need?

_____

_____

_____

MALCOLM

I have been carrying around this secret. I want to tell, but it's just that it's kind of an ugly thing, and I'm embarrassed. Okay…I got an "F" on my report card—actually two—and I was really scared to tell my dad. I know he would say, "Nothing is that bad," but he doesn't know how bad this is. The thing is, I just couldn't hold it in anymore. I was just feeling too awful. So, on my way home from school I decided today was the day I was going to tell him.

The elevator ride up to my third-floor apartment seemed to take forever. I walked in the door at three-thirty and he wasn't home yet. I looked in the fridge. Nothing. I washed my face, went back into the kitchen, and looked in all the cupboards, but there was nothing good to eat there either. I checked the fridge again, hoping something new and exciting would be there, but no. I paced back and forth, washed my face again, combed my hair. I was freaking out and didn't know what to do with myself. I was so angry—angry at myself. Have you ever felt like that? I wanted to do "the battery thing," but I decided I had to stop that, too. Stop getting "F"s and doing "the battery thing."

See, for about a month now I have found myself pulling batteries out of my desk drawer and throwing them out the window. It made me feel better, but I knew I was doing something really, really bad. I mean these weren't little triple A's; I'm talking D's here, and it became a habit. When I was done with all the batteries in my room I took the batteries out of the radios, the television changers, clocks, and flashlights. Things stopped working all over the apartment, and no one knew why, except me. It was like another dirty little secret, and I knew I had to stop. What I was doing made me think of the people who flew their planes into the World Trade Center.

Those men were probably angry too and didn't think how their angry actions would affect those they hurt and the people who loved them. I mean, I certainly wasn't thinking about that. All I knew was that I felt angry and that I wanted to feel better. But then I thought about what *would* have happened if one of those batteries hit somebody on the head or in the eye down on the street. I mean, I'm throwing them from the third floor of my apartment building.

So, when my dad walked in the door I sat him down, and he just listened to what I had to say about the grades. Then, I surprised myself because I went right ahead and told him about the batteries. That's when I really felt better. My dad said, "You know, Malcolm, I can see you have been torturing yourself over these things, so I'm not going to punish you. I think you have done a good enough job. But son, instead of being self-destructive, maybe next time you'll want to yell into a pillow."

I wasn't sure, but I thought I saw him smile as he walked out of the room.

EXTRA MONOLOGUE NOTES—MALCOLM

SEVEN KEY QUESTIONS—TYRESE

Who am I?

_____

_____

_____

Where am I?

_____

_____

_____

Why am I here?

_____

_____

_____

What happened right before (the monologue)?

_____

_____

_____

What do I want?

_____

_____

_____

Who am I talking to?

_____

_____

_____

What costume or props do I need?

_____

_____

_____

TYRESE

My best day ever? Oh, that's easy—when I met my dad for the first time. I mean, I had seen him before from afar, and had some cards from him and a picture of us when I was a baby, but I had never talked to him.

So, I went to go meet him in the jail he was in, and we talked for a whole hour, sitting on the picnic benches in the sun outside. We ate the McDonald's my auntie brought, and we talked, and it was great. He told me he loved me and would write to me. That was about…I don't know…five years ago. But I remember it as if it were yesterday. It's weird to think that in my whole time alive, all (*put in your age*) years, this one day could give me the most happiness. That one hour five years ago was the best time of my life, and I didn't really know that 'til just now, 'til you asked me.

And when I think about it, it's as though I'm back there again in some way. Like I get to relive that time in my mind or my heart. I don't know what part of a person remembers, but that memory totally belongs to me. It makes me think there must be many other things that happened just sitting inside me, happy things, just waiting to get fished out. Maybe the key was just being asked.

It's like a new door in me has opened.

But then this makes me think that there are bad memories too. I know there are more of those in me than the good ones, and I really don't want to remember them. Maybe the good ones were trapped under the bad ones and couldn't get out. Do you think you have to remember the bad to get to the good? Maybe there are no happy times without the sad and scary ones, because then you would have nothing to measure them by. I don't know. All I do know is that one hour was the best! Amen.

EXTRA MONOLOGUE NOTES—TYRESE

SEVEN KEY QUESTIONS—DEAN

Who am I?

_____

_____

_____

Where am I?

_____

_____

_____

Why am I here?

_____

_____

_____

What happened right before (the monologue)?

_____

_____

_____

What do I want?

_____

_____

_____

Who am I talking to?

_____

_____

_____

What costume or props do I need?

_____

_____

_____

DEAN

I had a bad day at school today. You know how it is. I mean classes were fine; nothing great. But at lunch, Dean, of course, came in with something new, except this time it was the new Puma basketball sneakers with the blue stripe. I was so pissed, man. He knew I wanted those. I told a few of my boys at lunch last week and, of course, he has to come in with them on. I don't think he would have ever even liked them if I didn't. So when we got on the basketball court for P.E. I taught him a lesson. The coach took me out for "inappropriate conduct" and "lack of team spirit."

When I got back to the group home where I live, a few of my friends at dinner asked how many baskets I scored. I felt really stupid that I didn't score any, because all my time on the court was spent checking Dean. Man, what a waste. It just doesn't seem fair that he gets everything and is a jerk too.

Every month the state gives me a certain amount of money that goes toward paying for my care at the group home, for clothes and extras like a movie or toys or candy. There is not a lot of extra, no matter what time of year it is. Even Christmas. I never, ever have anything I want. Maybe no one does, but Dean. But it was the last straw when he came in with those sneakers I can't have. I just couldn't stand it and had to whoop his butt. I know it was wrong, but honestly, he deserved it.

SEVEN KEY QUESTIONS—SECOND STRING

Who am I?

_____

_____

_____

Where am I?

_____

_____

_____

Why am I here?

_____

_____

_____

What happened right before (the monologue)?

_____

_____

_____

What do I want?

_____

_____

_____

Who am I talking to?

_____

_____

_____

What costume or props do I need?

_____

_____

_____

SECOND STRING

Me, Jason, Paul, and Justin have been best friends since the second grade. Our favorite sport has always been basketball. We were totally excited when the four of us got picked for the team. We love going to practice after school and then walking home afterwards. Our parents and teachers have always called us the four musketeers. So, today at practice our coach had Jason sit on the bench most of practice, and then announced who would be first string for our first game against the Marlborough School. This did not include Jason, which meant that for the first game of the season he would be sitting on the bench. We were really shocked. I mean, he is just as good a player as anyone on the team.

When we walked home we all said how unfair it was and that we would talk to the coach. Paul said he would sit on the bench instead. But Jason didn't talk at all. He just walked, looking down at his new hightops the whole time. When we got to his house he didn't even say 'bye', but just ran as fast as he could across his front lawn and then disappeared inside. Me, Justin, and Paul didn't understand how the coach picked him to be on the bench. We really thought he was just as good.

Paul heard that this happened last year to the Conover brothers. David played all season, and his brother Pete stayed on the bench. Now they aren't close like they used to be. We never thought it would happen to us. How is it that someone decides who is better? Who belongs and who doesn't? It never used to be like that. It used to be games were for fun, and everything was made equal. But now it becomes more like a competition. Who is in the higher math class, who scored higher on the SAT's, who got into the gifted school, won the award or made first string. I don't get it, and I hope I never do, if understanding means that I will start to measure others as better, smarter, or dumber because they add faster or throw a ball farther.

EXTRA MONOLOGUE NOTES—SECOND STRING

SEVEN KEY QUESTIONS—PEARL HARBOR

Who am I?

_____

_____

_____

Where am I?

_____

_____

_____

Why am I here?

_____

_____

_____

What happened right before (the monologue)?

_____

_____

_____

What do I want?

_____

_____

_____

Who am I talking to?

_____

_____

_____

What costume or props do I need?

_____

_____

_____

PEARL HARBOR

My grandfather was a surfing nut. He loved living in Hawaii because there were always really amazing new places to find beautiful, big waves. Any free time he had, he and his best friend, Martin, could be found in the ocean. Some people thought he and his surfing buddies were immature, but he felt different. He lost jobs because when the surf was good he had to go, no matter what the consequences. He was addicted. He said it was a good addiction for him and his friends, because it wasn't bad for your body; it made you stronger. He was at his happiest riding a wave and felt at one with everything for those few minutes. It gave everything meaning and put life into perspective for him. So, it made sense that the one job he loved was being a lifeguard.

He told me a story about the time he was in the Navy. On December 7, 1941, he got a call at his lifeguard post to come back to the naval base in Honolulu. He and his best friend, Martin, got in his Jeep and began to drive down Wainuenue Highway when they saw these airplanes flying low in the sky. As they drove on, the planes started making a booming sound. EEEERRROOO-RATATATTAT. And then holes appeared in the top of Grandpa's Jeep. They couldn't believe it.

Suddenly the sky darkened and filled with black smoke. Grandpa and Martin pulled the Jeep over and ran to the beach, where two planes had crashed into some battleships.

Hundreds of dead bodies were floating in the water. All the sailors were ordered to pull the bodies from the water and put them into caskets. There were so many that they were forced to put two bodies in one casket at a time—an American soldier and a young Japanese pilot, face-to-face in a casket together. It didn't make any sense to him. These two young people, the same age as my grandfather, didn't even know each other and didn't have a problem with each other. It was so weird and sad to my grandfather, who was such a peaceful guy, that the next day he protested against the war. He got a lot of support from the locals for speaking out against the government for what he believed in. But he was dishonorably discharged from the Navy.

He said when looking back on his life he felt good with his decisions. He based his decisions on what felt right to him rather than what society deemed right, and has never regretted it. I can only hope to be as strong when I become an adult.

EXTRA MONOLOGUE NOTES—PEARL HARBOR

SEVEN KEY QUESTIONS—CHADON

Who am I?

_____
_____
_____

Where am I?

_____
_____
_____

Why am I here?

_____
_____
_____

What happened right before (the monologue)?

_____
_____
_____

What do I want?

_____
_____
_____

Who am I talking to?

_____
_____
_____

What costume or props do I need?

_____
_____
_____

CHADON

Todd and I have been really tight for the first few months of school. I have never had a cooler best friend, except Greg, who moved away last year. I felt really lucky to find him. We like all the same hockey, basketball and football teams. Usually, if he's not doing well in a subject, I help him out or the opposite. He's usually really good at what I suck in. So, we always pick up each others' slack and never make fun of each other. It's like, "Come on, man, you can do it. Look, the common denominator is two, and this is why."

So the other day after school we both missed the bus. We walked about two miles to his house from school, and I was blown away when he started walking up the steps to one of the most beautiful houses I have ever seen. I just followed him and didn't say anything, but I thought it was like a joke.

His Mom greeted us at the door and said, "I'm so glad you boys missed the bus because I get the pleasure of meeting you, Chadon."

She was so polite and the house was unbelievable. There was a winding marble staircase, and it looked just like a museum, so clean and bright. Todd brought me to the kitchen, and there was a see-through refrigerator, filled with every kind of food you can imagine. He pointed at what he wanted, and the maid took it out and put it on plates for us.

I watched him as we ate, almost afraid that he wasn't the same person I'd known, the person who had become my best friend. But he was. As he ate he was no different—just as cool and relaxed as always. No attitude whatsoever. When we went up to his room to play, it was as big as the house I grew up in. I started thinking that I couldn't be friends with him anymore. He was too rich; we were too different. But the thing is we weren't different at all. I thought I would fall out when his mom came upstairs and said "Okay Chadon, it's getting late, honey, I'm going to drive you home now."

I didn't know what to do. I only knew how to get back to the home from the bus, and Todd didn't know that I was an orphan and lived in a group home. No one knew but the teacher, and I wanted to keep it that way. "No. I can walk, Mrs. Williams. Thank you, though."

"Walk? Why sweetheart, it's seven o'clock at night. Won't your mother be worried sick? Let me call her."

"No, ma'am. My mother won't be worried at all, believe me. I'm good at taking care of myself."

They both tried, but I just went into that zone I go into when I need to do something but don't want to or am afraid. I just get really quiet inside. I know what I have to do, so I stop hearing everything around me and I just go, like I always have. I just picked up my book bag, thanked them, and quietly walked out of that house into the night, relieved that my secret was still safe—for a little while anyway.

EXTRA MONOLOGUE NOTES—CHADON

SEVEN KEY QUESTIONS—MAX

Who am I?

_____

_____

_____

Where am I?

_____

_____

_____

Why am I here?

_____

_____

_____

What happened right before (the monologue)?

_____

_____

_____

What do I want?

_____

_____

_____

Who am I talking to?

_____

_____

_____

What costume or props do I need?

_____

_____

_____

MAX

Recently, I started my own business tutoring kids on the violin. My violin teacher of ten years suggested I do it. I charge fifteen for a session, which usually takes about an hour, unless someone is very slow. In a way this is a lot easier than being a counselor at my mom's camp because it doesn't take as much of my time…except, at camp I made a lot of extra money selling these (holds up liquid sour candy) at cost. It was good for three reasons: A) the money; B) endless supply of my favorite candy; C) I'm always in demand. A teacher of mine called me an entrepreneur. It means "One who undertakes to start and conduct an enterprise or business." And I think that is totally correct. I take what I like, for instance, the candy or what I'm good at, the violin, or teaching and organizing the kids at camp as a counselor, and make money with it.

See, "it"—that thing I do well—becomes a job. I guess I'm lucky at figuring out how to make money. People say it's because I know who I am, but to me it is just normal. I've always known how to make money, but that's what I do. It's not who I am. Now, my Uncle Jack makes money, all right, but he just can't keep a job. My mom is always saying that Uncle Jack can't find both shoes from the same pair. It bothers me when I hear my Uncle Jack say to my mother that he has always had trouble finding himself. But he has been there the whole time. He's looking around for himself, and he can't see because he's in "it"…inside himself. The way I see it, Uncle Jack hasn't lost himself at all. I think he's just confused between thinking what he does is who he is. I can think of lots of things he does well and could probably make money at. God, this is deep, man. I'll bet I could be a good guidance counselor, huh? Next career, what do you think?

EXTRA MONOLOGUE NOTES—MAX

SEVEN KEY QUESTIONS—ABOUT LESLIE

Who am I?

_____

_____

_____

Where am I?

_____

_____

_____

Why am I here?

_____

_____

_____

What happened right before (the monologue)?

_____

_____

_____

What do I want?

_____

_____

_____

Who am I talking to?

_____

_____

_____

What costume or props do I need?

_____

_____

_____

ABOUT LESLIE

So, we are at the Starbucks across the street from school, and I keep looking down at the smooth, yellow, wooden table. I'm feeling so lucky to be sitting across the table from her that I have difficulty looking at her. I had fantasized about this for so long—I guess part of me couldn't believe it was real. In my mind, I trace her with my eyes, starting at the perfect middle part of her hair, around her face, across her jade eyes, and then over the freckles on her nose and cheeks, down her mouth and neck, all the way to the thick, blunt, straight ends of her hair that always, always hit just below her boobs. I want to remember everything about this date. I want to photograph it in my mind so I will always have it—just in case it's my first and last time with her.

I move my hand back and forth, feeling the smoothness of the table again, and look out the window at the parking meter. She holds her hot chocolate with both hands like it's something very precious. It's cool, because I bought it for her and she seems to be enjoying it. Oh God, I want to drink from the same cup as her.

"Is something wrong?"

I shake my head.

"You keep rubbing the table."

I feel embarrassed. I guess she can tell; she smiles and reaches over and I catch her smell. She smells like, like the way flowers smell at night when I'm out walking the dog—very soft, beautiful, almost not there—that's what Leslie smells like. Unbelievable. She puts her hand on top of mine and I feel that touch everywhere.

But something *was* wrong. I had worried that I wouldn't do good on the date because everything was falling apart in my life. I wanted to say that I found out yesterday that my parents are getting a divorce. I wanted to tell her that I couldn't figure it out. I never even heard them argue. And I wanted to tell her my dad said they kept their problems to themselves because they didn't want us to hear them yelling. On top of that, my oldest sister, Alena, just moved back into the house with her baby because her jerk boyfriend won't marry her. How my mom is a lunatic, my dad doesn't care, and how there's no more money left.

That's what I wanted to say, until I realized that Leslie was holding my hand. I was so afraid that I'd say the wrong thing that I missed the moment. You know? When I realized that and looked at her too, that's when the date really began.

EXTRA MONOLOGUE NOTES—ABOUT LESLIE

SEVEN KEY QUESTIONS—THE LONELY MOMENT

Who am I?

_____

_____

_____

Where am I?

_____

_____

_____

Why am I here?

_____

_____

_____

What happened right before (the monologue)?

_____

_____

_____

What do I want?

_____

_____

_____

Who am I talking to?

_____

_____

_____

What costume or props do I need?

_____

_____

_____

THE LONELY MOMENT

I was reading this book by Deepak Chopra last night called, "The Seven Spiritual Laws of Success." I mean, I'm (*put in your age*) and I can't even tell my friends, the few I have, that I'm reading this book because they won't get it. I don't say that to be condescending, but it's true. People always say to my mom or me, "Well, *you're* so lucky *you're* so bright." I mean, my teachers want to move me three grades ahead, but my parents feel that would isolate me further. So, I am home-schooled. This has worked out well intellectually. I don't have to hide what I know by keeping silent, so I'm not seen as a showoff. It was a hard balance before at school.

Anyway, something I read stayed with me. The author asked why, if someone says you look handsome today you feel happy and seen. But if someone says you look tired and worn out today, you feel ugly or down? Why can certain words or the ideas behind them give or take away so much? I mean, aren't we the same either way, and still handsome?

So I go back to my first point: Why would someone feel bad if they are told they are average and supposed to be happy when they are tested and proven super bright? I would give my left pinky to be able to be like everyone else for a week. So next time you give someone a compliment, I ask you to consider both sides of it.

I know my knowledge will benefit me more when I'm older, but life is made up of moments, and it's this moment that counts. This lonely moment. I have probably about two million hours 'til I'm eighteen and in college, finding my own people. And people say childhood years are the golden years. Well, I don't agree.

EXTRA MONOLOGUE NOTES—THE LONELY MOMENT

SEVEN KEY QUESTIONS—KEVIN

Who am I?

_____

_____

_____

Where am I?

_____

_____

_____

Why am I here?

_____

_____

_____

What happened right before (the monologue)?

_____

_____

_____

What do I want?

_____

_____

_____

Who am I talking to?

_____

_____

_____

What costume or props do I need?

_____

_____

_____

KEVIN

The most amazing thing happened today. I was standing in line at the student store and saw Veronica, one person ahead of me. Her hair is this incredible sandy color, and I know it sounds silly, but I know her hair and hands and her back so well because I have made a point to sit behind her since second grade. So, I have had a lot of time to study those parts that you might not think of as beautiful—but I do.

Like when we had art class last semester and were assigned to make clay sculptures. I chose to do Veronica, but from the back, and I didn't tell anyone who it was. My art teacher told me it was quite special, and that my attention to detail and the feelings she got from it made her know that I was very connected to the subject I sculpted. If only she knew how connected!

Anyway, I'm daydreaming into her hair of sand, and she turns to the person behind her and says, "You can cut in front of me." My heart was pounding; I couldn't look her in the eye. I didn't know she knew I was even there. She looked down the hall both ways, whispered in my ear, "I like you," kissed me on the cheek, pushed the door open to the playing field and walked out the door. The light and air hit me and then the door slammed behind her. I stood there in shock.

I kept playing the scene over and over in my mind because it was so great and such a surprise that my brain needed time to catch up to my heart.

That thing that happened took about thirty seconds. How can I describe it? It changed everything. My whole world is different now—better—the best. It's so weird to think that the words we say and things we do to each other can have such a big effect so fast. How cool is life.

EXTRA MONOLOGUE NOTES—KEVIN

SEVEN KEY QUESTIONS—JOEL

Who am I?

_____

_____

_____

Where am I?

_____

_____

_____

Why am I here?

_____

_____

_____

What happened right before (the monologue)?

_____

_____

_____

What do I want?

_____

_____

_____

Who am I talking to?

_____

_____

_____

What costume or props do I need?

_____

_____

_____

JOEL

My grandma has all of these sayings: "Know your chickens," "Too many cooks spoil the broth," "Don't count your chickens before they hatch." Her favorite, "It is both a blessing and a curse." These sayings were just like a line of words strung together, and never meant anything to me until now. It is so weird that all your life you hear something, and yet you never know what it means until something in you changes, and you begin to see everything differently.

You see, I had a best friend named Joel, and we did everything together. Told each other all of our secrets and went everywhere together. So when this new guy came to our school, he and Joel became like insta-friends, and suddenly I was completely out of the picture. I was so upset, confused and weirded out. I mean, why? I hadn't changed; it didn't make any sense, and he never even told me why. He just left the friendship. It was totally awful, because he also happened to be my only friend.

Well, out of nowhere the cutest girl in my class, Hannah, told me how sorry she was about Joel. She sat with me at lunch and stuck up for me when a few of the guys made fun of me in gym class. I couldn't believe it. I mean, at this age it's usually like the girls against the boys unless you're sporty. Anyway, we started to hang out more and more and talk on the phone almost every night. She told me all her secrets, and we spent all of our free time together. At one point, Tara Melner went to sit next to me in math, and Hannah said, "I was sitting there," and Tara goes, "Oh, next to your boyfriend!" And without blinking an eye, she said, "No. Next to my best friend." It made me feel great and very special after the whole thing with Joel.

The next day, boys from the class who usually never talk to me and usually call me weirdo behind my back, started talking to me and asking to sit with me at lunch. So, I let them sit with me and Hannah. She was happy for me and so was I, until I realized that they were being nice to get close to Hannah. It was both a blessing and a curse, because I had begun to like them, and I think they had begun to like me. Only it felt a little weird because I knew it happened out of the fact that they were using me to get to Hannah. But by then it didn't matter. Then Hannah told me who she liked, which was hard, because while it was really cool that she trusted me it was really hard because I liked her and I felt kind of jealous. I mean, it was a blessing and a curse to be the best friend of the cutest girl in school, and a blessing and a curse that Joel stopped being my friend.

So, I think I will listen more carefully now when grandma fires out one of her sayings, wouldn't you?

EXTRA MONOLOGUE NOTES—JOEL

SEVEN KEY QUESTIONS—EDWARD

Who am I?
_____
_____
_____

Where am I?
_____
_____
_____

Why am I here?
_____
_____
_____

What happened right before (the monologue)?
_____
_____
_____

What do I want?
_____
_____
_____

Who am I talking to?
_____
_____
_____

What costume or props do I need?
_____
_____
_____

EDWARD

Have you ever had a day when everything goes wrong? I'm sure you all have; it's part of being alive, part of being human. But some days are just worse than others, ya know. Sometimes, I just do things wrong and I don't know why. I mean I know I'm hyper. I don't mean to be, and then I end up getting yelled at by my teacher and my parents and a friend, all in the same day, and it makes me feel terrible, 'cause I don't even know what I did.

Like today in class. I look over at my friend, Jennifer Constance, and she just makes me laugh. I mean she doesn't even have to do anything. She just has this super-alive energy, and I look at her and can't help but crack up. We always make fun of each other and try to get each other to laugh out loud in class. Today, I thought of something so brilliant it made me laugh just thinking about it.

See, Jennifer has these buck teeth. So I pulled out a sheet of lined paper and made these (he draws on paper a square with a line down the middle, cuts it out, and inserts it where his two front teeth are, like two big rabbit teeth).

So, Jennifer starts to laugh out loud, and the tears are running down my face from laughing so hard and keeping my mouth closed so the teeth don't fall out. And now other people see and are laughing, too. That's when Mr. Ravioli, my social studies teacher sends me to the office. I can't really blame him though.

To avoid further problems, I began my homework the minute I got home. I was really on a roll, and I looked up to find my thoughts and my eyes catch the hanging crystal my aunt Mary bought me. It is so cool how it casts a rainbow on my ceiling. I felt so lucky at that moment to have her as my aunt that I decided to call her up to tell her how much I love the crystal, and then she tells me something funny, and I'm hysterically laughing until I look up, and my parents are standing in the doorway, arms folded. They are furious, because I'm not supposed to be on the phone. It is homework time, and they also had heard about my brilliant idea with the teeth. So, they yelled—a lot. I said it wasn't my fault—I couldn't help it—I don't know why I am the way I am. One thing seems to flow into another, and it seems to be the opposite from the way I should be going.

"Mom, dad, I'll try harder to focus. Okay? I'm sorry. Do you want to see the teeth thing now?"

EXTRA MONOLOGUE NOTES—EDWARD

SEVEN KEY QUESTIONS—DEAD

Who am I?
_____
_____
_____

Where am I?
_____
_____
_____

Why am I here?
_____
_____
_____

What happened right before (the monologue)?
_____
_____
_____

What do I want?
_____
_____
_____

Who am I talking to?
_____
_____
_____

What costume or props do I need?
_____
_____
_____

DEAD

School: 7:30 a.m. A hand, with MUERTO tattooed across the knuckles, slams my locker closed before I can get my books out. I stare at the hand. My heart is pounding. I don't need to look at the face belonging to that hand. I know who it is. I don't look at the face belonging to that hand out of fear and respect. I hold my breath, afraid to move.

"Muerto is what you will be if you see Melissa again."

The hand disappeared, and I was left staring at my closed locker. He would kill me without a thought. I was warned out of respect. I know of other kids at school who have been stabbed, badly beaten up, and someone had a finger cut off for touching what was his with no warning.

I had dreamed of being with Melissa since I was a kid. Nine years later, I finally work up the courage to ask her out and now this. Last night was the best night of my life. Now I'm dead either way.

SEVEN KEY QUESTIONS—THE LONG WAY HOME

Who am I?

_____

_____

_____

Where am I?

_____

_____

_____

Why am I here?

_____

_____

_____

What happened right before (the monologue)?

_____

_____

_____

What do I want?

_____

_____

_____

Who am I talking to?

_____

_____

_____

What costume or props do I need?

_____

_____

_____

THE LONG WAY HOME

I took the long way home from school yesterday. A couple of guys from this gang, The Lords, had threatened to kick my butt after school for absolutely no reason. These guys mean business. It's not like I can reason with them, and I really didn't feel like getting cut from ear to ear.

So as I'm walking home, I pass a construction site that has been all boarded up. I was curious to see what was being built. I looked through one of the slats and saw like twenty guys standing in a circle in this pit, surrounded by lit torches. In the center two pit bulls were tearing each other apart. It was disgusting, and they were moving so fast it didn't look real. I had never seen two dogs fight like that. They were definitely trying to kill each other, and the guys in the pit just looked on and didn't do anything. I recognized some of the guys from The Lords and thought the other ones must be from a rival gang. Instead of killing each other they would have their dogs do it. I wanted to do something, but I knew I couldn't.

The smaller brown dog went down; his legs twisting in the air. The firelight from the torch made his eyes look red, and then the other dog bit into his neck. Blood squirted out everywhere; there was a loud yelp, and then nothing. I could still see the firelight in the smaller dog's eyes, but I could tell he was dead. It was like the light was only reflecting from the outside of him, not from the inside. It was weird. All the guys clapped.

I turned and ran home as fast as I could. It was like I was trying to run away from what I saw, but it was already in me. That night, I lay in bed and stared at the television screen. I felt too upset to turn it on. I thought, like all this life was going on inside the TV. All those channels, all those stories— too many to watch at one time. How I could flip through the ones I didn't want to see by just pressing a button. How I wished I could do that with the pictures of the dogs repeating in my head. I knew I was changed forever and it scared me. I closed my eyes and prayed for sleep.

EXTRA MONOLOGUE NOTES—THE LONG WAY HOME

SEVEN KEY QUESTIONS—COLEMAN

Who am I?

_____

_____

_____

Where am I?

_____

_____

_____

Why am I here?

_____

_____

_____

What happened right before (the monologue)?

_____

_____

_____

What do I want?

_____

_____

_____

Who am I talking to?

_____

_____

_____

What costume or props do I need?

_____

_____

_____

COLEMAN

The weirdest thing happened to me the other day. On my way home from school I thought I heard a dog crying. I looked around but there was no dogs anywhere. So I got home, put my book bag down and headed for the kitchen. I shuffled through the mail and saw that the divorce papers my dad had left were under the pile. I stared at his signature and the empty space under it where my mom was supposed to sign. I called out for my mom, but she didn't answer. I knew my dad wasn't around. He hadn't been home for a couple of days.

I was alone and I felt kind of relieved, like when you suddenly take a really deep breath and your whole body relaxes. It makes you realize you've been holding on tight everywhere but didn't know it.

I opened the cupboard and quickly took out the peanut butter, grabbed a knife and began spreading the peanut butter fast and thick on the Wonder Bread. I snatched a Hershey bar lying on the counter and unwrapped it at warp speed as I turned on the oven. I threw a few squares of the chocolate into my mouth and chewed hard.

My chest began to heave. I fell to my knees on the linoleum, weeping, open sandwich in one hand, Hershey bar in the other, and cried so hard I started sweating. I thought I heard the sound of a hurt dog coming from outside again. I stopped to listen but the whimpering stopped. The sound made me remember a time last year when my dog got hit by a car in front of our house. I guess that's what made me cry so hard.

Finally, I got up and opened the oven and put the open peanut butter sandwich on the grill, pulled the chocolate from the silver paper and put it on top and closed the oven. I grabbed a paper towel and blew my nose, took a chilled mug from the freezer, poured milk, and wiped my eyes. I looked outside to see if there was a dog, and then heard a key in the door. My mom walked in and looked at me.

"You okay?"

I nodded.

"You sure?"

"Yeah."

She walked to the dining table and picked up the divorce papers my father had left for her to sign. She stared at the first page for a long time and then at me. I turned back to the kitchen and rescued my burning sandwich. I kept listening for the sound of the dog, but it didn't come.

EXTRA MONOLOGUE NOTES—COLEMAN

GIRLS

SEVEN KEY QUESTIONS—STAR WARS

Who am I?

_____

_____

_____

Where am I?

_____

_____

_____

Why am I here?

_____

_____

_____

What happened right before (the monologue)?

_____

_____

_____

What do I want?

_____

_____

_____

Who am I talking to?

_____

_____

_____

What costume or props do I need?

_____

_____

_____

STAR WARS

It was my turn to clean out the class's rabbit cage. Someone fed Willy cabbage this week, so there was a lot of bunny poop pellets. It was a little grosser than usual, so I was happy when Todd Kreiger offered to help me. The only problem is, I know how much he likes me, so I almost felt bad 'cause it was kind of like using him. It's not that he isn't nice, and actually the smartest boy in my grade, but he is also the biggest geek. He looks a little strange next to all the other kids. You know that song, "One of These Things Is Not Like the Others"? Well, it was written for him. He has frizzy red hair; he's very, very tall and extra thin. He has long feet, hands, huge ears, eyes that kind of turn up at the corners, which really makes for a strange-looking package, like a paper doll with parts pinned on that don't fit right. My dad says he is going through a stage and will grow into himself, and when he does he will be a very handsome and good man. Well, that may be true, but I'm only in grade school, so what he will be in ten years doesn't much matter to me. That's eternity.

Anyway, we are cleaning out Willy's cage, and Todd says, "Dina, I have been working around my house doing chores for my mom for four months to save up enough money to take you to 'Star Wars,' buy you popcorn, soda, candy, and take you for pizza afterwards. Could you go out this Saturday?"

I was surprised and happy at the same time. Since first grade I knew he liked me because I always stuck up for him. The other kids would make fun of him and Robert Asherey. They were mean, really mean. So, I would stick up for him and that's how I got my nickname "Underdog," which I am proud of. But I never thought it would lead me here. I mean, my God, he spent four months working to take me out and give me everything on that date. But I also felt really weird and embarrassed. So I said, "Todd, that is so sweet of you and I would like to go, but my mom won't let me go out on a date yet. I haven't even been to a boy-girl party. I don't feel ready. But thank you so much for thinking of me."

I could tell he felt disappointed and embarrassed because his face and ears got very red, and I guessed that his face felt as hot as mine. He looked at me hard. I think to see if I was telling the truth.

He smiled and said, "Okay. Well, maybe next year." Then he put the bunny back in its cage.

Maybe a year can do a lot. I don't know. We'll see.

EXTRA MONOLOGUE NOTES—STAR WARS

_____

_____

_____

_____

_____

_____

_____

_____

_____

_____

_____

_____

_____

_____

_____

_____

_____

_____

_____

_____

_____

_____

SEVEN KEY QUESTIONS—THE GAP

Who am I?

_____

_____

_____

Where am I?

_____

_____

_____

Why am I here?

_____

_____

_____

What happened right before (the monologue)?

_____

_____

_____

What do I want?

_____

_____

_____

Who am I talking to?

_____

_____

_____

What costume or props do I need?

_____

_____

_____

THE GAP

(*Yells into open door on stage, then slams it and addresses the audience.*)

Fine! Then I won't go to the stupid party! Why can't I just wear what I want? I don't understand—this is my body! My Mom is always bringing home these really weird clothes or taking me to specialty stores where all the people are from Europe. I just want to look like everyone else and shop at the Gap, for God sakes. My mom insists I'm ahead of my time with these special clothes, but I don't want to be. I don't even know what that means—"ahead of my time." So, it's Julia's birthday and I was so excited to go.

When I got home from school my mother says she had a surprise for me and to go look on my bed. I ran upstairs and saw this thick, red-knit sweater with silver bears on it and red leggings with silver hanging bears on the cuffs. If that wasn't bad enough, there was a silver headband to go with it. I didn't understand what I was looking at. I had never seen anything like it before. It was hideous. And then a feeling of horror came into my stomach when I realized that this was my surprise and I WAS SUPPOSED TO WEAR IT.

Well, I stayed in my room for a while 'cause I didn't want to go downstairs. I didn't want to hurt my mom's feelings, because she was so excited, but I felt bad saying I was mad at her. I mean, after all, she did buy me a present—but it's never what I want. I was confused. So I went downstairs and brought the red outfit with me and asked her, "What is this?" She looked so sad I thought I would cry, but I was also very angry.

"This is the outfit I bought for you to wear to Julia's party."

"No way, Mom! I can't wear this, Everyone will laugh at me."

"They won't laugh and you will put it on now. How can you be so spoiled? Do you know what I paid for that? I got it from Little Royalty. It just came in from Spain. No one else will have this outfit. It is so special, damn it! Now put it on."

"I won't!"

"You will or you're not going to the party."

I ran upstairs, crying, and after a while I thought, "I'll put it on and she'll see how awful it is and not make me wear it." So I did. I was ashamed, standing alone in my own room; that's how ridiculous it looked. I looked so dumb; there was no way I could wear it anywhere. I marched downstairs and said, "Mom, I can't wear this."

"Why, sweetheart, you look so beautiful; that color is fantastic on your skin."

"No it isn't. I look like an idiot. Please mom, take it back. I'm sorry but I hate it. Why can't we just go to the Gap?"

"The Gap is common. Everyone wears the Gap. You are special; you're not like everyone else, and you shouldn't try to be."

"Yes I am, Mom. I am the same and I want to be like the other kids. What's wrong with that?"

"How spoiled you are. Upstairs, now. You are not going to Julia's party unless you wear that outfit, and that's it."

"But Mom, I know what I like."

"That's enough. Upstairs NOW!"

So I went upstairs to call Julia. (picks up phone)

"Hello, Julia it's me. I'm so sorry I can't come to your party, but I'm really sick to my stomach. Okay. Bye. Oh yeah, Happy Birthday."

EXTRA MONOLOGUE NOTES—THE GAP

SEVEN KEY QUESTIONS—THE WIZARD OF OZ

Who am I?

_____
_____
_____

Where am I?

_____
_____
_____

Why am I here?

_____
_____
_____

What happened right before (the monologue)?

_____
_____
_____

What do I want?

_____
_____
_____

Who am I talking to?

_____
_____
_____

What costume or props do I need?

_____
_____
_____

THE WIZARD OF OZ

What did I do last night? I performed *The Wizard of Oz* again for the thirtieth time. Anyway, everything was going great. I was having so much fun, and we got to the part where I call upon the flying monkeys to get Dorothy and Toto. We have this really great stage designer who made trap doors for the monkeys to come out of, like from the underworld. So, I'm supposed to sing my song and then say, "Monkeys come join me." And as they come from the trap doors under the stage the smoke machines blow smoke into the theater with them. It's very exciting. Well, I finish my song and I say, or really shriek, "Monkeys come join me!"

While waiting for them to come, I look into the audience with a snarl on my face and wait for that booming noise as the trap doors open and the swarm of monkeys surround me, waiting for my orders. But they don't come. So, I nervously yell the line again, "Monkeys come join me!"

They still don't come, so I look down at the trap doors—and nothing. I begin to freak out. I look over at Steve, the piano player, who looked terrified, so I pace the stage quickly and make up words:

"Dorothy, I will find you, and you won't be happy when I do and…uh…"

I just kept talking until Steve began to play my song again, only this time, it was twice as fast. I stared at him in shock and then started speed singing when suddenly I heard the boom. The smoke began to float around my feet and I ordered those lousy monkeys to "FIND DOROTHY!" And then I exited, stage left, fast.

When I got backstage I asked, "What happened? I was left out there like an idiot for like ten minutes! Alone!"

Stacey told me Jill Kallet had diarrhea all day and ran to the bathroom at the last minute, and Melissa went to get her because she had been gone a long time, and then Claudine's wing got caught in the trap door and we couldn't get out.

"There was so much going on we couldn't hear anything until the piano began your song again and we were like, 'Oh, my God, we missed our cue!'"

"Where the hell is Jill Kallet?" I asked.

Stacey said she left the theatre and it was a good thing because I looked so angry, she thought I could cast a spell on her. Just then I saw Wendy on stage, holding the bag I was supposed to take from her. I realized she wasn't saying anything or moving. I got closer to the wings and saw a look of horror on her face and realized that I had missed my cue. I ran on stage, grabbed the bag, and she said her line. For the rest of the performance I thought she was going to kill me, and believe me when I tell you, she could.

My thoughts went back to Jill Kallet, and then I felt bad, because she must have felt just exactly like I did. And I was definitely planning on making it worse. In that second I forgave her, and instead of being mad, I felt sorry. I could only hope Wendy would do the same for me as we took our bows.

EXTRA MONOLOGUE NOTES—THE WIZARD OF OZ

_____

_____

_____

_____

_____

_____

_____

_____

_____

_____

_____

_____

_____

_____

_____

_____

_____

_____

_____

_____

_____

_____

SEVEN KEY QUESTIONS—THE WAVE

Who am I?

_____

_____

_____

Where am I?

_____

_____

_____

Why am I here?

_____

_____

_____

What happened right before (the monologue)?

_____

_____

_____

What do I want?

_____

_____

_____

Who am I talking to?

_____

_____

_____

What costume or props do I need?

_____

_____

_____

THE WAVE

Have you ever wished to be in a different place in time? A few summers ago at camp, I was on the bus going to the most amazing amusement park called Story Town. I was sitting next to my very best friend, Hinda, and the bus was full of kids, yelling and laughing; everyone was eating candy. I should of been happy. But I remember feeling so totally sad, looking out the left side of the bus window at cows and farms, at the rolling hills of green and beige. I wished that time would fast-forward, and I would be much older so I wouldn't have to feel this way. I tried to talk myself out of it, saying I was sitting next to my best friend, who I could trust, and I was going to a fun place, but it did no good. It wouldn't help to tell Hinda, because how could she understand, when I didn't?

She looked so peaceful sleeping. I began to get so uncomfortable that I wanted to jump out of my own skin. I had to do something, so I turned around in my seat and waved to myself in the future. I told myself that when I remembered this moment and waved back at myself it would be in a happier time. (*The actress turns around in her seat and waves to herself*). Nobody noticed when I waved, and the silliness of it made me laugh. I mean, there I am, (*put your own age*) years old, waving to myself, wishing to be twenty or forty.

My laughing woke Hinda up. She smiled at me and asked, "How long 'til Story Town?"

"Another hour," I said.

"What are you thinking about, Claudette?"

"Time, and how glad I am you're my best friend." Then I waved at her. She smiled and waved at me and went right back to sleep.

EXTRA MONOLOGUE NOTES—THE WAVE

SEVEN KEY QUESTIONS—THE TRAY

Who am I?

_____
_____
_____

Where am I?

_____
_____
_____

Why am I here?

_____
_____
_____

What happened right before (the monologue)?

_____
_____
_____

What do I want?

_____
_____
_____

Who am I talking to?

_____
_____
_____

What costume or props do I need?

_____
_____
_____

THE TRAY

Have you ever done anything that's so embarrassing that you are even embarrassed afterward by yourself? Well, this was one of those times. See, there is this group of kids, and they just seem to do everything perfectly. The way they dress, how they walk down the hall, how they eat—they are even perfectly cool in gym class. It's like at the beginning of the school year, a handbook was given out about how to be a cool kid, and I didn't get the handbook. Maybe I was sick that day. Or when I was in the bathroom it was given out, and when I came back they had already run out of copies. I really don't know. But you get the picture.

So anyway, everything had been going much better for me. Lately, I feel more comfortable with myself and the other kids, and what happens? Lunchtime, I get my tray, and as I'm getting off the lunch line I lock eyes with Seth Gershin. He is only the most popular and good-looking boy in my grade. Sort of like a young Brad Pitt. Well, when he looked at me I felt like everything close in and I couldn't breathe. Something in me said, *No!* Breathe, smile, open up, show him how wonderful you are—and I did. I took a breath and smiled at him. He looked at me for a minute with no expression and then smiled back. I thought, wow, this is great. He smiled at me. So, I guess I got a little over-excited and I winked at him and continued walking. Well, I felt like a different girl. "Hello world, here I am!"

Next he is smiling and laughing in my direction, and so is everyone at his table—everyone in the lunchroom too. I thought they saw the change in me and were applauding for me, until Ms. Clemmons, the lunchroom attendant, came running toward me. She pointed to my chest, and I looked down to see that I had been holding my tray at an angle and spilled my turkey giblets, applesauce, and ice cream all over my favorite yellow vest. They weren't laughing with me; they were laughing at me. I was paralyzed. I couldn't move. Shock poured through me. Ms. Clemmons had to pry the tray from my hands.

As I ran from the lunchroom, she followed me and offered to wash my vest. I gave it to her but was too upset to say anything. Her look said it all; she understood and said nothing.

That night, after my parents went to sleep, I went outside and threw my favorite yellow vest in the trash can by the side of the house.

EXTRA MONOLOGUE NOTES—THE TRAY

SEVEN KEY QUESTIONS—GRASS IS ALWAYS GREENER

Who am I?

_____

_____

_____

Where am I?

_____

_____

_____

Why am I here?

_____

_____

_____

What happened right before (the monologue)?

_____

_____

_____

What do I want?

_____

_____

_____

Who am I talking to?

_____

_____

_____

What costume or props do I need?

_____

_____

_____

GRASS IS ALWAYS GREENER

Alyson always wants to come over and eat dinner at my house, because usually my mom orders out from the best restaurants in town and then puts my brother's, my father's, and my food on separate trays. And we each go into a different room alone to eat while watching TV, or sometimes talking on the phone. To Alyson this is really fun and special. To me it's regular and sometimes kind of lonely. Anyway, my parents nine out of ten times won't let me have anyone over, so Al has only done the tray thing a few times.

Well, yesterday my mom let me go home with Alyson after school. We were so excited. We even got to walk to her house from school, which I loved, 'cause my mom always picks me up, which embarrasses me. I want to walk or take the bus like everyone else. I know she's trying to be nice, but I hate it. So we are at Al's house and her stepmom, Vicki, asks if I want to stay for dinner. I really wanted to, so I called my mom to ask, and she said yes.

Al and I were in her room, making up a dance, when Vicki called us for dinner. When we went downstairs, I was so surprised to see the table set with lots of food and her whole family waiting for us. I just didn't get it. Was it a special occasion? I was unsure of myself. I didn't quite know what to do. Vicki said, "Bonny, sit here by me." I did, happily, and the food was passed around; each person took some and filled their plates. Everyone was talking and laughing and looking at each other.

I thought I had stepped into another world. Alyson apologized for the frozen fish sticks, and I said, "What, are you crazy? This is the best meal I've ever had. Your house is so much more fun than my house."

"No. I like yours better, Bon."

"No way Al, this is great. No trays, not alone. Lucky you."

EXTRA MONOLOGUE NOTES—GRASS IS ALWAYS GREENER

_____

_____

_____

_____

_____

_____

_____

_____

_____

_____

_____

_____

_____

_____

_____

_____

_____

_____

_____

_____

_____

SEVEN KEY QUESTIONS—JOHN WAYNE

Who am I?

_____

_____

_____

Where am I?

_____

_____

_____

Why am I here?

_____

_____

_____

What happened right before (the monologue)?

_____

_____

_____

What do I want?

_____

_____

_____

Who am I talking to?

_____

_____

_____

What costume or props do I need?

_____

_____

_____

JOHN WAYNE

Even as a baby I always loved westerns. John Wayne was always my favorite. I don't know why. I mean, Lizzy McGuire is great, and stuff on Nickelodeon is cool too, but for some reason reruns of John Wayne films and reruns of Bonanza have always been my favorites. My mother says that I was born at the wrong time, and that my true love is a cowboy in Montana somewhere, herding cattle, and when the time comes we will find each other. She is very romantic and believes in true love, even though my dad left us when I was one. She always corrects me and says he didn't leave you, baby, he left me, and there is a big difference. But honestly, I don't see one.

Maybe that's why I'll never forget my first week of kindergarten when I met Mr. Attone, the principal. I looked up at the door to see the biggest, most handsome man standing in the doorway of the classroom. He had on a suit with stitching around the lapels and really shiny cowboy boots. He looked and sounded just like John Wayne. He talked to the class for a while, but I don't remember anything he said. I just stared at him like I couldn't believe he was real. I started to pretend he was my father and he had his horse out in front of the school, waiting to take us on a ride. When he turned to leave the classroom I walked up to him, took his great big hand in mine, looked him square in the eye and said, "It is an honor to meet you, John Wayne."

His eyes lit up and he said, "It is an honor to meet you, Miss Kathy. Would you like to join me for a cup of tea?"

I nodded, and off we went to his office, where his secretary brought us tea and cookies and we talked for a long time. It was one of the best times I have ever had.

Before bed that night I told my Mom what happened. She took my face in her hands, kissed both my cheeks, and told me with tears in her eyes it was a sign that I will find my cowboy someday and all my dreams will come true. Then she tucked me in and turned off the light.

EXTRA MONOLOGUE NOTES—JOHN WAYNE

SEVEN KEY QUESTIONS—NEXT DOOR NEIGHBORS

Who am I?

_____
_____
_____

Where am I?

_____
_____
_____

Why am I here?

_____
_____
_____

What happened right before (the monologue)?

_____
_____
_____

What do I want?

_____
_____
_____

Who am I talking to?

_____
_____
_____

What costume or props do I need?

_____
_____
_____

NEXT DOOR NEIGHBORS

Just about every day I climb over the small fence connecting my yard and my neighbors' yard to visit my friends, Hilde and Norman. They are like my grandparents. I mean I don't have any, and their kids don't come to visit them, so it worked out perfect. I know that no visits from their kids makes them sad, because when Norman says, "Rudy is still in Vienna," or "Kirsten left a message," the left corner of Hilde's mouth curls down, and then she looks at her hands like she's making sure all her fingers are there. Norman's eyes well up with tears, and he immediately begins to search for his glasses. I guess that's why we kind of need each other.

They have this dog, Alice. She's white with black and apricot spots and a ring around her eye. Hilde and Norman say she's my dog, too. I'm glad, because I really love her, and I'm not allowed a dog of my own. Norman always shares his food with Alice, which I think it is so sweet. One day he was eating a Creamcicle and bit off small pieces, took them out of his mouth, and handed them to Alice. She loves anything cold, especially ice cream. My mother happened to see this and thought it was disgusting.

I had always had the feeling that my parents didn't like them, but I didn't know why. After that, my mom told me not to go over there so much; that I was probably bothering them. I told Hilde and Norman what my Mom thought. They both got on the phone and told my Mom that they loved me and looked forward to my visits and always had fresh milk and baked cookies waiting for me. I guess that made it okay, because she didn't say anything after that, until one warm summer evening, when Hilde and I took a long walk around the neighborhood. It was so beautiful out and we talked about everything. It was as if there was no time, and for some reason I felt closer to her than ever. It all felt very special. I don't even remember what we talked about, but I do remember how happy she looked, and that I can't remember feeling happier. When I got to the end of her driveway we hugged as always. I looked down at her tan-freckled arm and her hand holding mine, and she said, "Aufwiedersehn, my dear Esther," which means goodbye in German.

I walked up my driveway and saw two police cars. My mother sat on the ground in front of my house, sobbing. She looked up and I could see her hazel eyes were now a light green, which happened only when she cried. She ran toward me and shook me, yelling, "Where have you been? I have been worried sick!" As she spanked me I stared at the red flashing light on the police car and wondered what I did wrong. I told her I was just walking with Hilde and was so sorry that I scared her. She said, "You will never go over there again."

The next day a very high fence was put up between the yards, so high I could not climb it. I saw Hilde and Norman only one time after that. I was in the car with my family, going to synagogue. I waved to them from behind the glass of the back window of the car. They waved from the end of their driveway. As we pulled away I saw Hilde looking down at her hands and Norman checking his glasses, and I knew they were as sad as me.

EXTRA MONOLOGUE NOTES—NEXT DOOR NEIGHBORS

SEVEN KEY QUESTIONS—THE RECORDER

Who am I?
_____
_____
_____

Where am I?
_____
_____
_____

Why am I here?
_____
_____
_____

What happened right before (the monologue)?
_____
_____
_____

What do I want?
_____
_____
_____

Who am I talking to?
_____
_____
_____

What costume or props do I need?
_____
_____
_____

THE RECORDER

My cover is blown. In Mrs. Gilbert's class we have been learning the recorder for the past three months. We have to know five songs for our recital next week: "Go Tell Aunt Rhodie," "Claire du Lune," "When the Saints Go Marching In," and I can't remember the other ones—which doesn't surprise me, 'cause I can't play them either. Actually, I can't play any of them. Honestly, I have tried—pretty hard too—but for some reason, I can't remember anything that we learn. When I sit down to practice I don't know one hole from the next. My mother says it's because I'm dyslexic, and so I must try harder than everyone else, but I just can't get it.

So today in class Mrs. Gilbert says, "Okay class, it's recorder time. Time to get your instruments, sheet music, and take your places."

Luckily, even though I'm the smallest, my place is in the back row with my best friend, Rozlind Dandridge, who just happens to be the tallest girl in our grade. She is just the best, the funniest, and smartest, and plays the recorder so great that it makes up for my pretending.

But today it finally happened. The playing starts, and I do my usual thing of putting on a good show to make up for not playing. I think of it as my contribution. So there I am, next to Roz, and the class is blowing out, "Go Tell Aunt Rhodie," and it sounded pretty good. I'm moving my head side to side, smiling, moving my shoulders and hips…. I have this fancy move where I hold the recorder a little higher and throw my head back like an elephant would do with his trunk, and fantasize it's my solo, and for about a minute I get carried away. I believe that not only can I play the recorder, but I'm the best in the whole school, and I'm giving a recital all alone in the huge auditorium under the lights. Every seat is taken. They have all come to see me, but then the song ends, and we turn to the next sheet of music, and off I go again into my own world.

But today at the end of the song, Mrs. Gilbert put down her recorder and had tears in her eyes. She never looked like that before. I got kind of scared. She said, "It is rare that a student will come along with what we call talent, passion and just stands out from everyone else. Well, we just happen to be lucky enough to have one of those individuals here today."

Well, we got all excited and looked around at each other. Who? Who is this special person? Could it be Roz?

"Jill, will you please come forward and play for the class? Grace us with your enthusiasm and love for the recorder."

For a minute I forgot my own name, and looked at my classmates who were all looking at me, while I'm looking at them, trying to remember who Jill was, until I see Mrs. Gilbert staring at me. I couldn't move. My heart was pounding.

"Don't be shy, Jillybean. Come forward. I've seen you in the back row, knowing your love of music. Come to the front and play your favorite."

I moved to the front of the room, not knowing how I got there. It was like I wasn't in my body at all. I wondered how far I could take this. Maybe by magic I really could play; then

I thought of the big fat "F" that would be on my report card, and as if in slow motion I lowered Mrs. Gilbert's music stand and opened to "Go Tell Aunt Rhodie." With a very serious face I looked at the whole class. They were all so completely still; it was like time stopped in that classroom. All of them waiting for something so important to happen. And it was me they were waiting for. For me to give them something they needed.

I waited as long as I could, wondering if they could hear the thunder of my heart beating. I took a deep breath, put my lips to the mouthpiece, and looked at the first note. It looked like Chinese to me. I blew out a note. Just one. It quivered along with my lips.

I yelled out, "I can't!" and ran out of the room.

SEVEN KEY QUESTIONS—BUS STOP

Who am I?

_____

_____

_____

Where am I?

_____

_____

_____

Why am I here?

_____

_____

_____

What happened right before (the monologue)?

_____

_____

_____

What do I want?

_____

_____

_____

Who am I talking to?

_____

_____

_____

What costume or props do I need?

_____

_____

_____

BUS STOP

I haven't heard from Jason, because he's been grounded. So, when school was over today and I got on the bus, I was shocked to see him, sitting at the back with his friends. I stared at him for a long time. He didn't look at me, but I know he saw me. I sat with my best friend, Lisa, who is always hanging on him. Lisa told me to go sit next to him, but then said that she heard from his friends that Jason was going to break up with me. It was like the whole bus was staring at me, waiting for me to do something. Finally, I couldn't take it anymore. I felt weird. My heart was pounding so hard, fast, and loud that I thought everyone could hear it. I got up in what seemed to be slow motion; my mouth was so dry I was worried that I wouldn't be able to say anything. It was such a long walk from my seat to his. I sat down and said:

"Hi."

He looked so beautiful I couldn't believe it. I wanted so much to touch his hair and kiss his cheek, but I didn't dare.

"Hi," I said again.

He would not speak to me. He would not look at me. As we got closer and closer to my bus stop I was worried he would keep silent, and that the bus ride would end without him speaking, and I would have to spend all weekend replaying this horrifying experience over and over in my head until Monday. Embarrassed by everyone knowing what he was gonna do, and me being the last to know.

I felt a sharp lump in my throat rise, and my face got hot until I couldn't hold on any more. Then tears escaped, down my face, a lot of them. It was like in streams, and then snot came dripping out of my nose, just when we got to my stop. I blurted out "I LOVE YOU, JASON," and ran off the bus.

EXTRA MONOLOGUE NOTES—BUS STOP

SEVEN KEY QUESTIONS—TOMAHAWK

Who am I?

_____

_____

_____

Where am I?

_____

_____

_____

Why am I here?

_____

_____

_____

What happened right before (the monologue)?

_____

_____

_____

What do I want?

_____

_____

_____

Who am I talking to?

_____

_____

_____

What costume or props do I need?

_____

_____

_____

TOMAHAWK

(Actress sitting with a box of photos, a camp yearbook, and a ribbon won from a contest. She stares at the picture and then addresses the audience.)

I just found this picture of the horse from summer camp. His name was Tomahawk. I remembered how one day he got spooked and ran behind the barn. He was stuck between the back of the barn and the huge fence that separated the camp from the street. I could hear him whinnying, and I knew something was wrong because there was a crowd of campers and counselors around the riding area. I walked quickly to where everyone was and went to the riding teacher and asked what was wrong. She said he was out of control and acting dangerous, and they couldn't get him out from behind the barn. He had hurt himself from all the bucking and running and hitting the fence.

I walked to the front of the alleyway where he was. Both his legs were scratched and bleeding. His eyes were so wide you could see the white part on top. He whinnied again and threw his front legs up in the air. I became very calm and just looked at him. I knew he was terrified. He didn't know where he was. I don't know how I knew that, except it was as though he told me, but not in words. It was like he told me his thoughts in an idea or a picture. Anyway, I walked toward him slowly, speaking quietly, telling him it was okay, that he was all right, and not to be afraid; I wouldn't hurt him. I was his friend and would help him.

He blew out his lips and lowered his head to meet my hand. His nostrils were wide and quivery from breathing in and out so quickly. He lowered his head practically to the ground and I petted his sweaty brow and soft nose. I spoke quietly and asked him to follow me. He walked behind me slowly. The clopping of each hoof touching the ground brought us closer to his safety. The riding coach handed me his bridle. I put it on him gently and led him into his stall. I stayed while the vet cleaned his wounds.

After that I always rode him for all my lessons. I felt like I had a special magic, and the secret was listening to myself, trusting what I heard, and going forward without fear.

EXTRA MONOLOGUE NOTES—TOMAHAWK

SEVEN KEY QUESTIONS—GRANDMA

Who am I?

_____
_____
_____

Where am I?

_____
_____
_____

Why am I here?

_____
_____
_____

What happened right before (the monologue)?

_____
_____
_____

What do I want?

_____
_____
_____

Who am I talking to?

_____
_____
_____

What costume or props do I need?

_____
_____
_____

GRANDMA

The first time I flew on a plane alone I was in first grade. I had already traveled many times with my parents, to Hawaii, Arizona, California, Puerto Rico. But this trip was to my grandma's, who lived in Virginia. I was very excited but also scared. It was my first time being away from my mom except for a sleep-over. But this was definitely bigger.

As I got to the gate, a flight attendant took me from my mom and brought me to my seat on the plane. I had a bag of candies and a coloring book to keep me busy. At the first twinge of fear, I reached into the brown paper bag and pulled out the most beautiful hand-painted lollypop. That lollypop was so my mom. It was like a little piece of art, and immediately the tears started to fall out of my eyes. I knew if I kept staring at the lollypop it would make me miss her more, so I unwrapped it quickly and put it into my mouth. The sweetness helped. I asked myself why I felt sad and afraid, and it was because I was petrified that I would die in a plane crash and never see my mom again. I had never been afraid to fly before, so I told myself how much fun I would have with my granny.

The stewardess brought me a Coke and I started to relax—until I looked out my window and saw my mom, standing, looking out the huge airport window, eating malted milk balls. I could see her plain as day, even though there must have been five hundred feet between us. I waved, wondering if she could see me too. And then she reached under her glasses and wiped her eyes. Knowing she was crying made me cry also. She just looked so lonely.

The plane began to take off, which was a very good thing, because that is one of the most exciting things ever. Mom always said two of the most amazing things to her are how a big heavy plane can take off and fly and that babies can be born.

When I got to Virginia, I was so happy to see my granny. We went in her Duster (that's a car) to Williamsburg, which is like a colonial town. It is straight out of the 1920s or even before that. Everyone and everything looks like a colorful version of "Little House on the Prairie."

In one of the stores there were all these incredible bonnets. I picked a yellow one with tiny red and blue flowers, and granny got a light blue one. We laughed hysterically, trying them all. Before bedtime that night I went through granny's underwear drawer and laughed and laughed, trying on her huge bras and girdles. She came in and caught me and laughed too. "It's not nice to make fun of an old lady, Lizzy Lou."

We got into her huge bed. She put on the TV, and we ate Rocky Road ice cream with our bonnets on and laughed at our reflections in the mirror on her dresser. Soon granny fell asleep with her bonnet on. I watched her and felt really happy until I started to think about stories my mom had told me about how my grandpa used to beat my mom up, and granny would just stand by and do nothing or just walk away as if nothing was happening. My mom explained that at that time in granny's generation you didn't go against your husband. But it made me so hurt and angry thinking of my mom being hurt, and granny doing nothing!

I couldn't believe that granny and this granny were the same person. I became hot with anger, and before I knew what I was doing, I balled up my fist and punched my granny right on top of her head. Then I rolled over just as fast and pretended I was asleep. She woke right up and called out my name, but I didn't answer. I laid there with my eyes shut tight and heard her go into the bathroom.

I did feel bad, but also right about it. She deserved to get back a little bit of what my mom lived through for so long. The next day when she went out for milk I called my mom and told her. She actually laughed. She said it was a terrible thing to do, and to never do it again, but she understood why I did it and loved me so much. I felt better and thought maybe in some small way maybe I fixed the past by letting my mom know someone was there to fight for her here today.

SEVEN KEY QUESTIONS—AILEEN

Who am I?

_____

_____

_____

Where am I?

_____

_____

_____

Why am I here?

_____

_____

_____

What happened right before (the monologue)?

_____

_____

_____

What do I want?

_____

_____

_____

Who am I talking to?

_____

_____

_____

What costume or props do I need?

_____

_____

_____

AILEEN

On Valentine's Day, my best friend sent the boy she likes a teddy bear with a balloon attached. She was too afraid to tell him it was her, so she just wrote, Happy Valentine's Day. Signed, Anonymous.

We waited by the water fountain near his locker until he came to find the claim slip, telling him that there was something for him at the student store. When I saw him coming down the hall, a feeling went through me like electricity. My heart started pounding, and I whispered to Dana, "Here he comes." She looked at him quickly and squeezed my hand. I was so excited for her. She took a drink from the fountain to not be obvious.

He was wearing a green football jersey with the number twenty-four in gold. He had just had his dark brown hair cut shorter and very spiky. He looked beautiful. He pulled the ticket off his locker looked around, then turned and headed toward the store. We followed once he got around the corner, clutching each other's arms and giggling. When he got to the student store we went into the stairway to watch him. We could only see his back, but it told us everything we needed to know. We saw Ms. Everstein take the slip from Chris, disappear, and come back with the bear and balloon, smiling as she handed it to him. He read the card, sort of examined the bear, shrugged his shoulders and threw the bear into the dumpster and walked away.

Well, Dana and I had been holding our breath the whole time, and suddenly, after he walked away, we both took a breath, like out of shock. We were totally confused, and the pain in her eyes was almost more than I could bear. This was, after all, my best friend, and she was so hurt and disappointed. I felt helpless. This wasn't supposed to happen. So I said, "Dana, you didn't sign your name, so it's not like he's rejecting you."

"Yeah, but how could he throw a gift like that out? That's so cold, and what if I did sign my name, and he threw it out? That would be way worse. Forget it, I'm over him."

"But he doesn't even know you like him."

"It's over," she said. "I have to go to third period math. Thanks for doing this with me, Aileen. I love you, and promise you won't tell anyone, okay?"

"Of course."

Well, of course I wouldn't tell, but I knew I had to do something; it couldn't be over—not yet. So I went to Chris' best friend, Bruce Glazer, and I asked him if he knew if Chris liked anyone. Bruce got this huge smile on his face, and I thought, "Oh my God, he likes Dana." And he said, "Aileen, he likes you." My stomach felt like it was going to fall on the floor.

"Me?"

"Yeah, do you like him, too?"

"No. I have to go."

I don't know why, but I went back to the water fountain where Dana and I went earlier, to get some water and collect my thoughts, when I saw him coming down the hall again. Our eyes locked, and that same electricity went through me like before, and then I realized that I liked him too…more than any other boy. I was excited and miserable, because I knew it could never be, and because I could never tell anyone. For the first time in my life I felt totally alone.

SEVEN KEY QUESTIONS—JENNY

Who am I?

_____

_____

_____

Where am I?

_____

_____

_____

Why am I here?

_____

_____

_____

What happened right before (the monologue)?

_____

_____

_____

What do I want?

_____

_____

_____

Who am I talking to?

_____

_____

_____

What costume or props do I need?

_____

_____

_____

JENNY

From the first day I met Vicky and Missy, two years ago in Ms. Bollins' class, we put our desks together and wouldn't let anyone else join. Vicky and Missy have been my best friends ever since. But lately, Vicky and Missy have been spending most of their time hanging around Laurence Lupkin. So, I try to do it too, but I think he is just the most boring person I've ever met. He barely smiles and just exactly reminds me of a piece of cardboard or a robot. There is nothing in there; nothing is in or behind his eyes. It's very weird. But if they like him so much, I figure he must be great, and I'm not seeing it.

So, at free time I go over to where the three of them are by the book area, and I hear Laurence say, "Okay. Three o'clock Saturday, at your house, Vick?"

So, I say, "Oh, what's at three o'clock at your house?"

Vicky and Missy just looked at each other.

"What?" I ask.

And Vicky says, "Nothing."

"What's at three on Saturday, Vick?"

"Nothing you would like."

"How do you know?"

"It's just a small boy-girl party. A little get together. But there is no more room. My mom said only nine people. Sorry."

And they walked away. I couldn't believe it. I was being replaced by a piece of cardboard. How could they like him better than me?

A bus ride home can be a really, really lonely thing when you realize you don't have a best friend. When I got home I told my mom what happened, and she said that at a certain time boys become more important than anything. "If you were invited, would you have wanted to go?" she asked.

I thought about it for a while and said, "Oh, I wouldn't feel comfortable. I don't feel ready for a boy-girl party."

"Well, then, you shouldn't feel that bad, honey."

"But Mom, it would have been nice to at least be invited."

"Always nice to be invited, honey," she said, and she held me for a long time. I could tell she felt as bad as I did. I stared into her face and realized I didn't lose my best friend at all. She was right here the whole time.

EXTRA MONOLOGUE NOTES—JENNY

SEVEN KEY QUESTIONS—LAINIE

Who am I?

_____

_____

_____

Where am I?

_____

_____

_____

Why am I here?

_____

_____

_____

What happened right before (the monologue)?

_____

_____

_____

What do I want?

_____

_____

_____

Who am I talking to?

_____

_____

_____

What costume or props do I need?

_____

_____

_____

LAINIE

You know how brothers and sisters fight? How it is supposed to be like a normal part of growing up? Well, when I go to my friends' houses and see how they fight with their brothers and sisters, it makes me think something is not normal at my house. My brother terrorizes me. If my door is closed he kicks the door open and walks right in without knocking. When I tell him to leave he won't, and whatever I was doing he ruins it. Like, he will tear up my homework, rip my doll's head off, turns my heavy TV upside down so I can't watch it. He takes whatever I am eating, licks it, chews it up and spits it back on the plate. If I scream for my mother, he pulls my hair, hits me, and puts his hand hard over my mouth. We fight, and I always, always end up on my back, pinned down, my brother on top of me, laughing and kissing my face, as I squirm and struggle to get up. And he won't let me get up until I tell him that I love him. Then he always says, "You will thank me later. I am preparing you for the world, making you stronger." That's when I get so hot and angry I feel like I am going to break out of my own skin. My legs curl under and I am able to lift him off of me with my feet. After it's over and I finally escape, I always cry and tell him I'm sorry for hurting him. One time he kissed my mouth so hard my lip bled.

I know these are not kisses of love, because if it was love I would feel it. The kind of fighting we do makes me feel afraid to ever be in the house alone with him. Even though I told my mom, I still feel confused and embarrassed like I have a secret with my brother that I don't want to have. One time I got so angry from being held down that I bit his arm as hard as I could and waited for my teeth to meet. It was the worst feeling ever, because that was the time I learned what hate was. Yesterday, I finally asked him why he does this to me. He said it was because I had too much light in me and that he wanted to make it dimmer, and sometimes wanted to put it out altogether. Then he asked me why I would say sorry to him if he was the one hurting me. He always thought that was kinda of funny and sad at the same time. I didn't know the answer, only that sorry seemed to be the only thing to say after feeling so much hate for another person, especially when that person is your own brother. He just stared at me. I think this is the first real talk we have ever had. Maybe it will help. Maybe my mom will let me put a lock on my door. I hope so.

EXTRA MONOLOGUE NOTES—LAINIE

SEVEN KEY QUESTIONS—FIRST LOVE

Who am I?

_____

_____

_____

Where am I?

_____

_____

_____

Why am I here?

_____

_____

_____

What happened right before (the monologue)?

_____

_____

_____

What do I want?

_____

_____

_____

Who am I talking to?

_____

_____

_____

What costume or props do I need?

_____

_____

_____

FIRST LOVE

Loyalty has always been a big part of my nature, even when I was in Mrs. Lostrangio's class in first grade. I was madly in love with this beautiful boy named Arthur Bent. He had sandy blond hair in a bowl cut, but it looked excellent on him, and big blue, cat-like eyes. He was tall and always wore these light-blue and white running sneakers. I just thought he was amazing. We were both very shy, but were definitely in love. Looking back I can honestly say that the depth of love I felt for that boy is just as strong as any love I feel now as a (put your grade) grader. Anyway, I thought about him all the time. I would write his name and my name in a heart everywhere. He was always in my dreams, and I would fantasize that we would be at a dance or at our wedding in every detail. I never told a soul—not even my mother—'cause I knew she would make fun. I knew he felt the same way. The looks we would give across the classroom said everything. It was like I had known him forever, and before that too.

One day, my best friend Nancy Rudy, who was not really such a nice person but the most exciting friend I ever had, told me that she and Arthur liked each other. Well, my heart just about broke into three pieces on the spot. I asked her how she knew Arthur liked her too. She, who liked a new boy every week, I thought, could not possibly understand a boy as deep, intelligent, and princely as Arthur.

"He told me," she said.

I thought I would die. I mean, after all, he never said that to me. I guess I had been wrong all along; that it was simply my wish. So I said nothing. I watched her flirt with him all week and thought I would be sick. I got very quiet and every time I would watch her talk to him he would be looking at me. I thought he was just feeling sorry for me. It was truly one of the most miserable weeks of my life, until we had library time.

I took my book and went off to a table by myself. I just couldn't bear to see them together one more minute. I opened my book to find a Curious George bookmark in it with the words, I LOVE YOU, JESSE. I LOVE YOU, JESSE. I LOVE YOU, JESSE written all over the bookmark. My heart was pounding as I read each one, and when I got to the bottom it said, Love, Arthur.

My heart was racing. I couldn't stop smiling, so I closed the book with the bookmark inside, held it to my heart, and put my head down on the library table to hide my smile. I thought about our secret love, and that it had been real all the time. That's why I keep this bookmark to remind me that my feelings didn't lie to me.

EXTRA MONOLOGUE NOTES—FIRST LOVE

ABOUT THE AUTHOR

Elizabeth Bauman divides her time among acting, teaching, writing, and drama therapy. She has been teaching acting for the past ten years, both privately and at the Lee Strasberg Theatre and Film Institute in New York and Los Angeles. She also teaches at Scott Sedita Acting Studios, where she is the head of the Children's Department.

As an actress, Elizabeth has performed on both coasts at South Coast Repertory, Spanish Repertory Theatre, Circle in the Square, Provincetown Playhouse, the Matrix Theatre, and Marilyn Monroe Theatre, to name a few.

She received her Bachelor of Fine Arts degree in theatre from New York University's Tisch School of the Arts, a Master of Arts degree in educational theatre from New York University, and holds a certificate in drama therapy from the Drama Therapy Institute of Los Angeles.

As a drama therapist, Elizabeth works with underprivileged youth in group homes, developmentally disabled children and adults, as well as children with autistic spectrum disorders.

She currently resides in Los Angeles.

For more information
Please visit www.youngactorsworkshop.com.